Val

Goodness, Grief, And Me

A Daughter's Journey Through Love, Loss & Learning to Live Again

With love

Hilary Steel

Hilary xx

Perstone Press

For permission requests, please contact:
Hilary Steel
hilary@hilarysteel.com

Cover design: Suzanne Steel
Editing: Anthony and Margaret Smith
Printed in the United Kingdom

This is a work of nonfiction. Names, places, and events are portrayed to the best of the author's recollection. Certain identifying details have been changed to protect privacy.

First Edition 2025

Contents

Dedication 1

Introduction 3

How to Use This Book 7

1. Once Upon a Time 9
2. Meet The Parents 19
3. The Relationship Shift 27
4. The Transition 35
5. The Emotional Shift 41
6. I Don't Care 47
7. Self Doubt 55
8. My Incident 61
9. Caring Without Losing Yourself 67

10.	Healing Work	71
11.	The Goodbye Years	75
12.	Life After Death	83
13.	The Gifts of Grief	89
14.	Goodness, Grief, and Me	93
15.	A Note from Me to You	97
16.	Practical Exercises	99
17.	The Letter	107
18.	What 'Now' Looks Like	113
Acknowledgements		117
19.	Quick References	119
About the author		121

Dedication

For Harry and Jennifer, the parents who encouraged me to walk my path.

My brother Lindsay, who died while I was writing this book.

Everyone who walks through the fog of grief, searching for the way back to themselves.

"Grief is the price we pay for love." Queen Elizabeth II.

Introduction

Pleased to meet you. I'm Hilary, 53 ½ at the time of writing this. A girl who still gives her age in that way and who still counts down to important things in *sleeps.*

I spend a lot of my time talking about life, love, and loss, often all in the same sentence. As a funeral celebrant, I've stood beside hundreds of families as they've said goodbye to someone they love. Every service I write is a story, full of laughter, memories, and the little details that made that person who they were...warts and all. These stories could be in their own book...if they weren't private!

But when my world shifted, when grief came knocking loudly at my door, it was an experience that changed me, not just personally, but professionally too. I now realise that understanding grief from the outside differs from living it. As a result, I wanted to truly *understand* grief in all its forms: the chaos, the tenderness, the way it quietly rewires who we are. So, I studied to be a grief practitioner. It gave me tools and language to explore what had once just felt like fog, and it helped me support others in a deeper, more compassionate way.

This book, *Goodness, Grief, and Me*, began as my attempt to make sense of it all. It started with scribbles in a notebook and a few raw stories I wasn't sure anyone would ever read. Yet here we are, and I thank you for turning these pages.

How many times do you grieve *before* someone dies? The words poured out between care visits, hospital appointments, and long nights of 'What now?' This was my therapy. My way of making sense of a world that suddenly didn't make any. The pages of my journal were messy and disorganised, but I captured what I was experiencing at the time it was happening.

Over time, it became something more — part memoir, part guide, and part conversation about what happens when life changes, and how we somehow learn to live around the silence lurking in empty spaces.

Grief transforms you. And it isn't something that you can avoid. Once you meet grief, it remains a part of you, and accepting that it's something you can't change paves the way towards healing. My interest in healing slowly grew into something that is now almost a part of everyday life.

Grief is messy. It's unfair. But it's also proof that we've experienced love and that love also gives us strength, although it may not seem like it. If you've found your way here because you're caring for someone, because you've lost someone, or simply because you want to understand grief a little better, welcome. I hope that in these pages you'll find honesty, humour, and a little light — even on the darker days. Because **goodness, grief and ME**... we now know each other rather well.

This is my unfiltered story, the caring years, the losses, the breakdowns and breakthroughs. You'll also find the insights and practices that I wish I'd known about back then. These come not simply from textbooks, but from lived experience, later combined with the frameworks I use today as a celebrant and grief practitioner.

Each chapter tells the truth. Sometimes bluntly, often with humour, but you'll also find sections called **Practitioner Reflections** at the end of many of them. Think of them as conversation pauses, places to breathe, to learn, and to remember that what you're feeling isn't only normal, it's necessary. There's no script for coping with what life throws at you in these situations, but there are things you can do both to ease and to understand the intensity of what you are feeling.

I hope this book helps to see that grief isn't just about endings. It's also about how we can adapt to new beginnings.

Hilary

How to Use This Book

Just as grief doesn't come with a set of instructions to follow, neither does this book. You don't have to read it in order and can dip in and out, depending on where you are right now. ***The Practitioner Reflections*** are designed to encourage you to think a little deeper, without putting pressure on yourself. ***The practical exercises*** at the end of the book are gentle ways to work through what's tangled in your head.

Please don't rush; let the chapters sit with you, even if it means closing the book and picking it back up later. There's no finish line, so take small steps towards understanding yourself and how loss is affecting you. Awareness often signals the beginning of change.

Sometimes it creeps in, other times it bounds in like a wave you didn't see coming. The more honest you are with yourself about where you are, the more this book can signpost you towards those softer memories that offer comfort.

Once Upon a Time

Once upon a time, there was a little girl who lived a happy life with her loving family. As a child, she had the freedom to explore the world as she saw fit, muddy knees, bruised shins, and an understanding of time that meant *I'll be home when I'm hungry*. She was encouraged to grab life with both hands, even if that meant climbing the wrong tree, one far too high for her little frame (literally and figuratively!) or scraping her way into a new adventure. With three older brothers to learn from, some things she got up to didn't impress her parents, but she was free to make her own choices, and mistakes, from an early age.

That little girl was me. The above paragraph may sound *idyllic,* and in many ways, it was. Every traditional story has a beginning, middle and end. This is my story, spanning almost a decade of my life, nearly a fifth of my time on this planet. It's the story of love, loss, and the chaos that happens in between. And yes, despite the title *Goodness, Grief, and Me*, I promise you it's not all doom and gloom. There's plenty of laughter, a few swear words, and more cups of coffee and glasses of wine than any one woman should rightly consume. Some of my coping mechanisms at the time may not have been conducive to a level head, but they got me through.

Life started out in a market town in Lincolnshire where my parents (you'll meet them properly in the next chapter) owned a restaurant. I credit my love of cooking and entertaining to the hours I spent annoying the kitchen staff, wanting to *learn* about food. A curious toddler, they likely celebrated when it was time for me to go upstairs to the little flat for an afternoon nap. (Something I'm once again partial to!)

My first real memory of feeling something intense goes all the way back to infant school, again to do with food. School lunches were what nightmares are made of for me. I shudder when I remember the lunch supervisors forcing me to eat cold custard. I've never been a pudding person and being made to sit in a nearly empty dining hall, staring at a jam roly-poly drowning in that thick, lava-like yellow sludge, brought out the rebel in me. (Cue tantrums)There was another girl in the same boat — only hers was the main meal she refused to eat. (We could have been best friends if we'd simply swapped plates.)

One day, she got lucky and wasn't kept behind. I was left alone, watching the staff tidy up, when one of the supervisors suddenly shouted to her colleague. Ever the nosy child, I looked over just in time to see them rush to the spot where the girl had been sitting — her entire plate of food had been scraped onto the floor. I giggled. I never found out what happened to her, but I remember thinking she was brilliant. In that moment, I couldn't help but imagine how good my custard would have looked under the table too. Fifty years on and this still haunts me. Not long after this my parents announced we were moving down to Kent. I had no idea where Kent was, but it was positive in my mind. The next day at school, I didn't care about the custard, only about this nightmare in my life would soon be over. Spoiler alert, at junior school the same thing would happen only this time about donuts!

Some may not see this as trauma...but for me, it was! Trauma is relative. It can come from a single shocking event or from years of smaller hurts that slowly wear away at your sense of safety. The school dining hall was *never* a safe space for me, not until we were allowed to bring a packed lunch that is. For one person, it might be the loss of someone they love: for another, it's being made to feel invisible, unheard, or unworthy. Trauma can live in the body, in memories, or in the way we react to things that seem harmless to everyone else. It's not always dramatic or obvious — sometimes it's that heavy feeling you can't explain, but it's there all the same. In my opinion, grief is the same.

When people hear the word 'grief,' they often brace for tragedy. But I'm a firm believer that we are, at least partly, the authors of our own endings. Life throws us plot twists we didn't audition for, but we still get to decide how we carry them, and how much we let them *define* what happens next.

So no, this isn't a sad book. It's real to me. It's about caring for my elderly parents for eight and a half years following my Mum's paralysis from a stroke. It's about how life can change in an instant, and how we all have no choice but to adapt to a new way of life. Those eight and a half years were tough. I learned a lot. Then in August

2019, my Mum died, followed three months later by the love of her life, my Dad. These pages are about the long nights, the laughter that sneaks in when you least expect it, and the strange, intense love that only comes when roles reverse and you're suddenly the adult in the room. Not a role I excel at, even now.

There were days when I felt I was absolutely nailing it, and others when I was crying in the loo wondering if anyone else had ever lost their patience with their mother *while simultaneously making her a cup of tea, exactly the way she liked it!* (Spoiler: they have.)

Four times a day, two people, (carers) came into my home. Some were brilliant, and others quickly discovered the role wasn't for them. I admire people who work in the care industry; they have a lot to deal with, and they are pivotal to the comfort and dignity of the people in their care. We worked out that during those years we had over 12,000 care visits to the house. That's a lot of feet traipsing over the carpet. It became as downtrodden as I was.

There were moments I cried tears of frustration, yes, but also moments of pride, ridiculous humour (such as when I stood behind her wheelchair at the top of a hill, joking about letting her go to see if she could break her previous record for speed. A lady standing near looked at me as though I were some kind of monster. We laughed.) and the resilience that sneaks up on you when you're too busy getting on with things to notice it forming.

This is what those years looked like — the lessons I didn't ask for, the love that kept me standing, and the strange new identity I had to forge after they were gone. This was difficult for me as I didn't have a clue what my 'new normal' would look like, or even what I wanted it to look like.

Although everyone's journey is unique, there's a camaraderie between people who've cared for their parents. A quiet nod between those who've changed dressings, managed prescriptions, and hidden their exhaustion behind a brave smile. We are the unsung heroes who give time, our patience, and sometimes our sanity, all in the name of love. Was it out of duty? Partly, but the love was still there.

If you're one of us, you may recognise yourself in these pages. And if you're not, you might still find something here about resilience, change, and what it means to truly show up for someone else.

Back then, life really was simple. It was the 70s after all. The restaurant was a great place to grow up. I stole cigarettes from behind the bar and copied what I'd seen adults do. Put one in your mouth, light it and puff away. I tasted beer from the pump, found the Babycham bottles and drank a few like pop, and ate *posh* food from the à la carte menu. My parents, Harry and Jennifer, were my *safe space.* They believed in letting us kids find our own paths, discovering independence. But they also believed in family meals around the table, proper conversations and always wearing your best underwear...just in case! As a child, if ever I said I was *bored,* I could guarantee being handed a feather duster faster than I could backtrack. It's a word that's still omitted from my vocabulary.

Looking back on that time now, I realise that the 'ordinary' world I lived in was actually 'extraordinary.'

And then *everything changed*. At 47, there was no way I could have predicted just how much this *change* would affect me.

When you're a child, you don't imagine one day becoming the adult who has to parent your parents. It's not a role anyone prepares you for. There's no manual, no practice round. One moment you're having lunch with Mum, chatting about both the important and the unimportant, and then you're trying to remember where near the hospital you've parked the car.

But this chapter isn't about loss. Not yet. That comes later. It's remembering what came *before* everything changed so dramatically. The foundations. The noise and the chaos that filled my family life before the silence crept in. It's about the love that was so clear because without understanding its depth I couldn't make sense of the grief that follows.

My parents gave me a solid grounding; the sort that's built around practical kindness and support with all the random and sometimes wrong decisions I made. Mum, who was 5ft 3 inches could command attention purely by raising an eyebrow. Dad was calm, a loyal family man, occasionally infuriatingly stubborn, but his heart was huge and his humour dry. I have inherited traits from both.

They taught me that *home* isn't just a place; it's a feeling, and this is something I held on to when the time came for me to care for them in their final years. I didn't know it then, but a lot of what they taught me would become part of a toolkit I used that got me through the hardest decade of my life.

If I could go back and whisper something to that younger version of me, the one who thought the world would always make sense, I'd say:

'Hold on tight. You're going to need that humour, that stubborn streak and that deep-down strength. They'll save you time and time again.'

So, what follows this chapter is a collection of messy truths, randomly remembered emotions, and one woman's clumsy but heartfelt attempt to do right by the very people who gave her life.

Practitioner Reflection: The Power of Before

When people talk about grief, they often start with the loss itself. But as a grief practitioner, I've learned that our healing begins by honouring *what came before.*

The "before" is where our roots are. The relationships, routines, and love that defined us.
It's important to spend time there. To remember the smell of the Sunday roast, the sound of your mum's laughter, or the way your dad's jacket smelled faintly of soap and his signature aftershave.

Grief doesn't erase these moments; it asks us to carry them forward. Before we talk about endings, let's first revisit the beginnings.

Meet The Parents

Harry and Jennifer Steel, born in 1931 and 1935 respectively. They met in a dance hall in Glasgow in the mid-1960s, back when people met on the dance floor rather than on an app. From that moment, their lives merged, and they remained together until the end. For over fifty years, they were a true partnership and loved each other so deeply.

Harry had gone to the dance with a friend who knew Jennifer. When the night wound down, she offered them both a bowl of spaghetti Bolognese in exchange for someone fixing her broken toilet. Harry was an engineer with a 'give me five minutes and I can fix that' kind of mind, and a home-cooked meal was too good an offer to pass up.

That's how it began. One dance, one repair job, a home-cooked meal and a lifetime of love. They were a couple who did everything together, bickered occasionally, but never fought.

They married, built a home and Harry welcomed Jennifer's two sons from her first marriage, Steven and Lindsay, into his world. Then came their two children, Mark, and then, finally, me. Mum always said she got it right in the end. (If my brothers are reading this, yes, that's exactly what she said.)

They named me Hilary, which comes from the Latin word for cheerful. I'll take that. After three sons, Mum was delighted to have a daughter. She had romantic ideas about dressing me in frills and bows and brushing my hair into neat styles with ribbons. Unfortunately, I was bald until I was five, and when I finally grew hair, the tantrums I threw as she tried to style it using her pink curlers eventually worked, and she gave up trying to mould me into her vision of a little girl. I was usually halfway up a tree or knee-deep in mud. Dresses were impractical for a life of adventure, so she gracefully surrendered to the tomboy phase.

Despite those early fashion disappointments, we made up for it later. As an adult, I became much more 'girly,' and she loved helping me pick out clothes or shoes, until I became a hoarder of different coloured Converse trainers to match every outfit! One thing she couldn't accept was my ordering a pint of lager instead of a 'much more ladylike' half-pint in the pub. She didn't drink, didn't smoke, and I did both.

I grew up as part of the generation who drank water from a hosepipe. When freedom meant your parents telling you to be home 'when it's getting dark'. We made our own entertainment. At home, you mucked in with the chores and did as you were told.

I was a happy child. I loved books, loved spending time alone, and was often under the duvet with a torch lighting up the pages of my latest adventure. Being told to 'go to my room and think about what I'd done' wasn't exactly a punishment for me.

They were close, funny, and affectionate. They made marriage look easy, though I'm sure it wasn't always. Watching them together made me believe in a love that lasts. (And yes, I did eventually find my person too. Her name's Sue, and she'll appear a little later.)

Dad was my hero. He had a calm way about him and could defuse almost any situation. I adored my dad and was proud to be a 'Daddy's girl.' I remember one cold evening, when I was about nine years old, walking through town and hiding inside his coat, my head just touching his waist while he guided me through the crowds. A protector.

Mum was the spark. Small but mighty, sharp as a tack, and blessed with a laugh that could fill a room. We shared a special bond that only deepened as I got older. We talked about everything, even the bits that made me cringe. She wanted me to grow up strong, independent, and kind...and she never let me forget my worth. I'll always be grateful for this.

She could also make you feel *seen.* When she listened, she *really* listened. Saturdays were our day. Even if I'd been out late the night before, I'd get up and take her to the market, then lunch in town. Those moments, those simple ordinary Saturdays, are what I miss the most.

My parents were in love, and more importantly, they *liked* each other. Mum told me that Dad was her priority in life, then her children and then the rest. To some, this may sound harsh, but I understand it more than ever now. If we focus on our relationship, then everything that surrounds it flourishes.

They were also wonderfully supportive. When I announced at seventeen that I'd like to move to Rome for a year to work as an au pair, they didn't stop me – they didn't even try to talk me out of it. I think they were too shocked. It wasn't exactly just up the road. Seven months after my announcement, they waved me off at the top of the drive as a friend drove me to the airport, hearts breaking behind encouraging smiles. This was the summer of 1990, before mobile phones, so communication was through letters and the odd expensive call. I still have those letters, tucked away for a rainy-day reread.

Rome was an amazing experience. I was fortunate to be with a wonderful family who treated me more like a fifth child than anything else. My first time away from home influenced so much, from my choice of degree, career and, more importantly, my love of Italian food!

When I came back to the UK, I went to the University of Kent to study languages. Mum was bursting with pride. She'd always wanted me to go, and I think she told every person she met her daughter was 'at university in Canterbury'. (Cringe)

During those years, we grew even closer. She'd call the porter's lodge to leave a message for me to ring her, and we'd meet for lunch in the city. We were what I call 'compatible eaters.' We could share anything on a menu, meaning we could taste more dishes. Those lunches were our catchups, our mother-daughter therapy sessions, our giggle breaks from life. On the day I graduated from Canterbury Cathedral, I honest thought she'd faint with overwhelm.

She was proud of me, and I was proud of her. She never infiltrated my life; she waited to be invited to see the parts of it I wanted to share. This probably drove her crazy at times!

Dad was my steady anchor. He was always there in the background with a practical solution or a sarcastic comment. At every netball tournament when I was at school, Mum yelled at the umpire to blow the whistle, Dad with a hipflask of something 'for the cold.' They were a team. The simplest of memories mean so much to me now.

When they both retired, they spent winters in Spain, then Malta, making friends and enjoying the sunshine. But we had one rule: no matter where we were in the world, we would always spend Christmas Day together. And we never broke that rule. I was fortunate to spend 47 Christmases with them, and that time of year is the *one* thing I *have* to know what the plans are, even more so now. Spontaneity is my middle name, but not when it comes to Christmas.

Mum wrote a cookbook in the 1980s, *The Great Potato Cookbook*. She was so proud of it, and so was I. A copy still sits in my reading nook, a small reminder of her creativity and drive. Yes, it looks dated, but some props used in the pictures I still use now. We scoured boot fairs together on Sunday mornings looking for *curiosities* that would look good in the images. The royalties from her book paid for holidays and other fun things for us all.

Looking back, what I see most clearly is how they raised me to be independent but to remain connected, strong but soft. We respected each other as individuals, not just as family. That balance is rare, and I'm so grateful for it.

But then came the night that changed everything. The night our family roles shifted and would never be quite the same again.

Practitioner Reflection: Remembering the Whole Story

When we talk about grief, we often zoom straight in on the loss itself. But the full picture of a person— who they were, how they lived, the joy they brought us — it's what grounds us.

If you're grieving, take time to remember things about the person you love. It's often the simplest of things that will make you smile in their memory.

Write details: the foods they loved, the jokes they told too often, the phrases that made you roll your eyes. These memories aren't side notes; they're the threads that keep love alive, long after loss.

The Relationship Shift

It was the middle of the night at Maidstone Hospital. The corridors were cold and too bright, the light that makes everything feel slightly unreal. I was standing there, trying to stay upright, when a man walked past and gave me that look — the look only someone else in the same boat gives you. No words needed, just that silent, exhausted understanding.

A few doors away, my mum, my 'Little M,' was lying in a hospital bed after what they suspected was a stroke. She was admitted by ambulance two hours earlier. I was still trying to catch up with what was happening.

Hospitals have their own rhythm. By the time the sun comes up, everyone else has somewhere to be. The nurses are rushing; the trolleys squeak down the corridor, and life carries on for everyone except you. I stood still while the world moved around me, invisible to everyone trapped in their own thoughts. I should add that the after effects of the alcohol the night before we beginning to take their toll.

By that afternoon, Mum seemed brighter. She was alert, cheeky even, demanding a *proper* cup of tea and something decent to eat. When she introduced Dad to the doctor as 'her boyfriend,' I felt a flicker of relief. Her humour was intact. Her spark was still there.

The doctor said she would be discharged the following week. 'Five sleeps,' Mum repeated, with only a slight slur, and Dad's whole body relaxed. We all clung to that number like a promise. Five sleeps and we'll be home.

But just one sleep later, our lives changed again.

That evening after we'd left, Mum suffered a major stroke on the ward. This one didn't play fair. It left her paralysed down her right side, and for a while, I thought I'd lost her completely. We knew nothing about it until we went to visit the next morning. 'F**K' was my first word when I walked in. She hated me swearing.

I remember staring at her, lying in that bed, and feeling as though I was outside my body watching someone else's life from a distance. She was so still. But then she looked at me. And her eyes — those sharp, expressive eyes told me she was still in there. She couldn't speak, couldn't move, but she was present. That look told me so much.

The next day. I made a makeshift communication board out of cardboard with letters and numbers. It was simple enough, but complicated at the same time. In the end, we settled on a simple system. One blink for yes, two for no. It was primitive, but it worked. It also led to some hilariously confusing conversations. At one point she was trying to tell me about another patient who had annoyed her, and between all the nods for yes and head shakes for no's, we were laughing like kids. I didn't need to understand every word; I just needed to know she was still *here*.

A few weeks later, it was my thirty-ninth birthday. I'd already organised to host a 'Wig Party' at a pub before the stroke and was ready to cancel. It didn't sit right to celebrate something when Mum might not see her next birthday. Sue convinced me to go ahead, that we needed to have something to look forward to. Before the party, Sue and I stopped by the hospital in full fancy dress.

Think vampire vixen with a black and red Gothic-style dress. Mum's face was priceless, a mix of disbelief and that classic 'are you really going out like that?' look she'd perfected when I was a teenager. But she smiled, and for a moment it was just *us* again.

She looked sad when we said goodbye. I think that's when it hit me: she missed her normal life. She wasn't the only one.

It took a while before I thought of myself as a carer. At first, I was just 'helping Mum and Dad'. But as the months went on, everything had shifted. Mum needed help with almost everything, and Dad needed help too, though he didn't admit it. He quietly stopped driving, and I quietly took over. He'd say, 'You enjoy driving anyway,' to save face. That was Dad, proud and dignified.

During those first months, our family dynamic twisted into something new. Mum wasn't caring for Dad anymore. Dad was doing his best to care for Mum. And I was caring for them both.

There was only one day during her stay in Maidstone Hospital that I didn't visit because I had a high temperature. It didn't develop into anything more than a day of sniffles, probably because I was run down.

Once, as I was leaving after a visit, she said, 'You'll look after your dad, won't you?' and I nodded. I didn't realise that for her, it was her way of preparing for a long-term farewell. I didn't consider what was going on in her mind.

Outside my family life, other things changed too. Some friends stayed close; others drifted. People don't always know what to do when illness lingers. I learned the hard way that I couldn't control how others reacted. The only behaviour I could manage was my own. I let people down by cancelling invitations at the last minute. Then the invitations stopped coming. Once I accepted that, it became a kind of freedom. My world shrank, and I clung on to everything that was important to me, and nights out in town didn't appeal any more.

Hospital visits became part of my daily routine, as did all the running around picking up things she needed or wanted. Then there was Dad; he was lost without my Mum, and he needed my time too. Mum had always taken care of everything at home. He was the practical, hands-on one of the team, and she took care of everything else. Subconsciously, I fell into that role at home, and to be honest; I wasn't brilliant at it. Things were neglected, but I always made sure he had clean clothes and three meals a day.

It wasn't easy. The line between daughter and carer blurred until I couldn't tell where one ended and the other began. But even then, I fought to keep seeing them as my parents. I didn't want our relationship to become purely functional. I still needed to be their child sometimes.

And that's the thing no one tells you. When roles reverse, you grieve *before* you lose them. You grieve the version of them that could make the tea, tell you off, and wrap you in a hug that said everything would be fine. You grieve the safety of being the one who's looked after. I didn't see this as grief, but it's exactly what it was. Grief for things that are no longer the same.

Standing in that hospital corridor, I didn't know it yet, but that night marked the beginning of a whole new kind of grief, the slow, living kind that changes everything.

Practitioner Reflection: When Roles Reverse

One of the hardest parts of caregiving is the moment we become the adult in the relationship. It can feel like we've been cast in a play without a script. This is what's known as **anticipatory grief**— mourning the loss of someone while they're still here. It's normal to feel resentment, guilt, sadness, and love all at once. It doesn't mean you're ungrateful or weak. It means you're human.

If you find yourself in this space, remember that caring for someone doesn't erase your right to *feel*. You can love deeply and still long for your old life. Both can be true.

This is an exercise that helps you check in with where you are right now.

Grab your 'comfort' drink, find a quiet space and ask yourself:

What hurts right now? What makes you feel better? What can you leave until tomorrow? Next week? What needs to be done now?

Understanding what you are feeling *in the moment* helps you to focus on one thing at a time, both emotionally and physically.

The Transition

June 2011. After three long months in hospital, Mum finally came home.

She was desperate to be back in her own space. I warned her that things might look a little different, but I needn't have bothered. The moment she rolled through the door, she clocked every change we'd made. Admittedly, some weren't to her liking, but most of the changes were purely functional. It was like battling an obstacle course to get her in the house because the house was deemed fit for purpose, without a way to get her wheelchair in or out! The Ambulance crew initially hesitated. I cried. They lifted her wheelchair up the steps.

Sue and I had worked ourselves to the bone getting the house ready. We'd rearranged furniture, set up her bedroom downstairs, and made sure the equipment was all in place. We weren't professionals; we were two women winging it with enthusiasm and a lot of love. But we did alright, and Mum's smile when she saw it made every bit worth it. There were some logistical issues that came up, but as soon as they did, we dealt with them. We were all learning to adapt together.

Dad was relieved to have her home too. He handled her not being there well, but it took its toll on him too. Even though she depended on everyone else now for almost everything, he still treated her like his 'darling girl.' That never changed.

Mum and Dad lived with Sue and me and bringing her home was wonderful but also terrifying. It was also incredibly disruptive to our every day lives and took a lot of juggling, spinning plates and making it up as we went along to make it work.

There's a kind of safety within hospital walls. When you're suddenly the one responsible for making sure they don't fall, choke, or forget their medication, the weight of it hits differently. I was trying to be positive, but inside I was panicking. How were we going to do this? How was I going to work, take care of Mum, and somehow keep our lives from collapsing into a rota of laundry, medication charts and panic? I succeeded and I failed, but I'm still able to laugh when I look back on the *chaos* that was *my life!*

Mum hated relying on others. She'd been fiercely independent her whole life, and I could see in her eyes how hard it was to let us take over. I didn't ask how she felt; I didn't need to. We both knew the answer, and neither of us wanted to speak it out loud.

Sometimes threw snappy comments, or words laced with frustration and fear. I was tired, resentful, overwhelmed, and the wrong tone of voice from anyone could set me off. Then I'd feel awful. The guilt hit harder than the exhaustion. I worried she thought I didn't want to look after her, when really, I was just scared I wasn't doing it well enough. Guilty as charged.

And here's the thing about guilt, it loves company. It hangs around, whispering all the things you *should* have done better, even when you know you were doing your best. Even recently, thoughts like this crept unwelcomed into my mind. I can't stop them, but I can stop them amplifying.

It's only now that I can see how much she protected *me*. She must have worried constantly about being a burden, but she never said it. She just waited until I came back home, gave me one of those looks that says, 'I know,' and we carried on.

As her care needs increased, so did Dad's. He started struggling quietly in the background, pretending everything was fine. I took over everything in the house — the cooking, the washing, the endless lists of appointments. I was juggling two versions of care at once: emotional for Dad, physical for Mum.

It's strange how fast 'helping' turns into 'full-time caring.' One minute you're leading a normal life, the next you're Googling 'pressure sore prevention' at 2 a.m. (Please don't Google this kind of thing unless it's necessary!)

Through all this, Sue was my lifeline. She had every reason to run a mile, but she didn't. We found our rhythm as a couple inside a house that never really slept. Some nights, we'd sit on the sofa with a glass of wine, laughing at the absurdity of it all, because if we didn't laugh, we'd cry. She was the person who took care of me. She was the one who kept our life ticking while helping dig me out when I was knee-deep in duties. Sue and I have been together for nearly twenty years at the time of writing this and I can honestly say, when you find 'your person' cherish them.

People would often say, 'I couldn't do what you're doing; it would drive me mad.' I'd smile politely and think, *yes, it might. But you'd be surprised what love lets you do.* It wasn't a choice to be in this situation, and we were fumbling along in the dark. But we did our best. Sue and I faced challenges head on. We didn't know what the hell we were doing, but we did out best.

It was messy, exhausting, and sometimes thankless, but it was also precious. I learned to celebrate the small wins: a smile from Mum, a calm afternoon, a meal around the table reminiscent of years gone by.

We became a strange little unit. Not quite traditional, not entirely functional, but we made it work.

Over time, the chaos became a kind of normal. The sound of carers coming and going, the whirr of medical equipment, the constant lists. It wasn't the life I'd imagined, but it was ours.

And through it all, I learned this: transitions don't happen in one big moment. They creep up on you. One day you realise the old version of your life has quietly dissolved, and a new one has taken its place.

Practitioner Reflection: The Quiet Shift

The transition from 'daughter' to 'carer' often happens in small steps. You rarely notice it until one day you realise your life revolves around someone else's needs.

In grief practice, it's called a **living loss** — losing the life you knew, even while the people you love are still here. It's normal to feel anger, exhaustion, guilt, and gratitude all tangled together.

If you're in that space, try this:

Pause once a day and name one thing you've done right. It doesn't have to be heroic. It might be making a cup of tea or sitting quietly beside them. That's care, too. Time is truly the greatest medicine and gift you can give to someone.

The Emotional Shift

If you asked me how I was doing back then, I would have lied to you. Offering the automatic reply of 'I'm fine' with a smile on my face. Then made a joke, maybe even convinced you. I'd say how grateful I was that Mum was home and doing well, how Dad was coping, how everything was under control. I believed it, or at least, I needed to.

But that wasn't the truth. Far from it.

Underneath the lists, the medication and the endless cups of tea, I was running on fumes. I was scared, tired and emotionally frayed and worse still, I didn't want to admit it. Saying it out loud felt like failure.

When trauma hits a family, it eats away at the foundations first. Ours had always been strong, but when Mum had her stroke, everything changed. Suddenly, I was the one holding it all together, and I wasn't sure I had the strength. She was the matriarch, the glue that made things stick.

I didn't want to be the matriarch. That was *her* job. I wasn't ready to fill her shoes.

In truth? I wanted my mum back. Not the version who needed hoists to get her in and out of bed and help with every other need, but the one who told me off for swearing, laughed at her own jokes and made Christmas magical.

But grief doesn't arrive all at once. Sometimes it starts long before death does. It seeps in quietly when you realise the person you love will never quite be the same again. That's what was happening to me; I just didn't have the language for it yet.

I remember meeting a woman by the hospital coffee machine a few weeks after Mum's stroke. She was visiting her own mum and told me she'd been caring for her for eight years. Eight? I couldn't wrap my head around that. How did she cope with dedicating eight years to the situation? I felt *pity*. I swore a lot in the conversations in my head. 'What the Fuck?' on repeat.

Wasn't this all a temporary blip? I couldn't imagine that this would be our life for longer than a few more weeks. I smiled at her, said something polite, and went back upstairs. But her words hung around and haunted me for weeks.

Eight years. Could I do that? Would I *have* to do that? ('WFT' once again)

Dad was changing too. He'd always been good under pressure, but as time went on, he became quieter, smaller somehow. His health wasn't great, but he never complained, well not about his health. He'd happily complain about insignificant things. He hid behind jokes, letting me take the lead with any decisions. I could see his pride and pain in equal measure. He still wanted to be her protector, but the roles had shifted, and we all pretended not to notice.

I tried to hold everything together, but my own emotions were like a washing machine on a never-ending spin cycle. Some days I was angry, some days numb. Sometimes I'd burst out laughing at something completely inappropriate. There were moments when I felt like two people, the practical, capable Hilary who got on with it, and the silent, crumbling one who just wanted to run away.

I've since learned that's what grief does to you when it's *still happening*. You can be functional and falling apart at the same time.

I buried my feelings for as long as I could, thinking I was being strong. But burying emotions doesn't get rid of them. They just wait patiently until the pressure builds, and then they come bursting out, usually at the worst possible moment.

I'd snap at Dad, sulk with Sue, or slam a cupboard too hard. This wasn't about the cupboard, of course. It was about the sheer weight of trying to be everything to everyone.

Over time, I learned to stop fighting my emotions, breathing through them instead of stuffing them down. I tried meditation. I read about grief and caring for elderly parents, about control, about letting go. I learned that it's okay to have contradictory feelings. You can love someone and still find the situation unbearable. I read the words, but they didn't always sink in.

This doesn't make you heartless. It makes you human.

There was a point, probably a couple of years in, when I finally realised this wasn't a short term thing. This was our life now. The care routines, the exhaustion, the emotional rollercoaster - all of it. I was trapped.

But somewhere, with that realisation came a strange peace. I couldn't change the present, but I could change how I handled it. Or at least, I could try to. I tried, failed and tried again. This was a pivotal period in my life, only it took until much later to realise it.

That's not to say I floated around full of Zen calm - far from it. But I understood my emotions weren't the enemy. They were the map, the one that would guide me truthfully, if I paid attention to them.

Practitioner Reflection: Naming the Storm

One of the most powerful things I've learned in grief work is that emotion itself isn't the problem; avoidance is.

When we try to stay 'strong,'we often push our feelings underground. But what we bury doesn't disappear. It waits.

If you're caring for someone or grieving someone still living, take a moment to name what you feel. Literally name it.

Say, "I feel angry." Or 'I feel trapped'" Or 'I feel love and resentment in the same breath.'

You don't have to fix it; you just have to see it, acknowledge its existence.

Once a feeling is recognised and understood, it loses some of its power to knock you off your feet.

I Don't Care

When Mum came home, everything revolved around her. Of course it did. How could we improve her life? What did she need? What had we forgotten? Every decision felt like a test, and Sue and I were the ones trying to make sure we passed.

Dad, born in 1931, was a gentleman of his generation. He believed in taking care of his wife, in sickness and in health. He adored her, and his world began and ended with her. If she was comfortable, he was happy. If she was struggling, he felt it too.

They were still as close as ever. Sometimes too close. They'd fall into their own private conversations, and I'd have to leave the room because there are some things a daughter does not need to hear her parents talking about. Their bond was still there, and it was beautiful.

But as much as I loved them, I hadn't signed up for this. I didn't want to be a caregiver. It wasn't part of my plan, and I didn't know how to do it. I wanted my freedom back. I wanted to travel, work, laugh, live. Instead, my life had become one long to-do list.

I am not a natural 'domestic goddess.' Far from it. I easily step over a pile of clean laundry on the stairs without seeing it, ignore the washing up for days, and forget a load of clothes in the machine until they smell suspiciously like old cheese. I'm not proud of it, but it's true.

And then there were the moments that tested every nerve. I don't like hair. Never have. I can't even watch someone brush it without a shiver. So, when Mum asked me to wash and set hers, it was like asking me to tap dance on ice (I do still own a pair of tap shoes and a practice board.)

We bought one of those contraptions that attaches to the hairdryer with a plastic hood that inflates around your head. She looked like an extra from *Doctor Who*, but she didn't care. I'd wrap her in towels and a bin liner, fill a bowl with warm water, and try not to gag when the hair came loose from the brush. She knew exactly how much I hated doing it but was so grateful.

When her hair was clean, she always smiled, showing me how much better it made her feel. And every time, I felt a sting of guilt for having moaned about it. She never complained, even when I dragged my feet. She just waited until I made the time to do it for her. Afterwards, seeing how much better she felt, in came the guilt that it hadn't exactly taken me long to have such a positive impact on her. A few years later, a friend at the time who was a hairdresser came round and between us, we even managed to perm her hair. I am grateful to that friend. She helped make a chore I hated into another laugh shared in the chaotic house.

Sometimes, frustration got the better of me. I was tired and scared and didn't recognise the life I was living. I missed the version of myself who wasn't constantly on call. Some nights I'd lie in bed, wide awake, thinking, 'I can't do this anymore.' And then morning came, and I'd get up and do it anyway.

One day I went to the GP for a check-up. My blood pressure was through the roof. The nurse looked alarmed and told me I needed to go to the hospital immediately. I laughed. 'That's not happening; I've got too much to do.' She made me promise to buy a home blood pressure monitor and let the surgery have my results. Thankfully, it turned out to be stress and what she called ‘white coat syndrome.’ Still, it was a wake-up call. My body was shouting what my mouth refused to say: I was swamped with overwhelm.

Fear became a constant companion, and not one I’d choose to raise a glass with. I was terrified of getting it wrong. Terrified that I’d make a mistake that would hurt them. Terrified that I’d snap one day and say something I couldn’t take back.

Sometimes I’d look at Mum and think, ‘What if she dies while I’m not here?’ Then I’d look at Dad and think, ‘What if he does?’ There was no room to relax. I was always waiting for the next crisis. I’m not being dramatic here. They often looked like they were close to dying.

It’s easy to talk about love in the abstract, but in practice, love can be confusing and inconvenient. I loved them both; of that there was no doubt, but there were moments when I wanted to scream. That’s the truth of caring that no one likes to say out loud. You can adore someone and still need a break from them.

Sue kept me sane. She had her moments of frustration too, but she never made me choose between her and them. We joked about living in a never-ending episode of *Groundhog Day*, and that humour kept us going. If you can laugh while filling out a repeat prescription form, or queuing to buy incontinence pads, you can survive almost anything.

The question that kept circling in my mind was, 'Why am I doing this?' Was it duty? Love? Fear? Or because I'd promised, years ago, that I'd never put them in a home?

It was all those things.

I didn't know when I made it, but that promise would come with a cost. It meant I carried the weight of being the one who had to make everything alright, even when nothing was.

Still, I never regretted keeping them at home. I just wished I'd known how to care for myself at the same time.

I mention the word *dignity,* and to see my mum's own cast aside was horrific. In those early days, she had a rota stand to help her move from the bed to the chair and back again. But there was also a dreadful contraption called a hoist. Watching it in use convinced me it was the most undignified and impersonal way to move someone. The straps were placed beneath her, then the mechanism lifted her and swung her across to the bed or the chair. Of course, then someone would lower her *safely.* But seeing Mum suspended in the air, terrified and helpless, was utterly heart breaking. We campaigned to have that thing removed before it stripped away what little dignity she still had. A year before Mum died, a lady came to the house with a clipboard clinging to her as though her life depended on it. Before she set foot in Mum's room, she'd already made the decision that a fixed hoist would have to be installed from the ceiling. I stood my ground, spouting off about dignity and how would she like it? I was furious but controlled my temper and didn't lash out at her. And the 'report' she was due to send with her recommendations, thankfully, never arrived.

Being a carer made making plans almost impossible. Spontaneity went straight out the window, unless it could be a week on Thursday at 7pm and only last for 28 minutes! A cheeky weekend away required military-level planning. Thankfully, Sue understood. If we braved it and went somewhere, she'd help me plan every detail, so nothing was left to chance. Asking others to help was hard. I knew my parents' routines, how they liked things. And then came the gloomy thoughts of 'what if something happens while we're away?' You get the picture.

My advice to anyone finding themselves at this stage is simple: don't sell yourself short. You already have far more of the right skills than you realise, and just by taking this on, you're doing something remarkable. Whether your caring role takes an hour a day or fills every waking moment, it's still your precious time. Time you're choosing to give to someone who needs you. And hopefully someone who appreciates you. Try stepping into their shoes for a moment. How must it feel to be in their position? What small things could make life easier? Both for them, and for you? It's the little things that can make an enormous difference.

Practitioner Reflection: The Myth of Selflessness

Caring often gets wrapped in the language of sacrifice. People say, 'You're amazing, I don't know how you do it,' and you smile, even though inside you're crumbling.

Love doesn't require you to destroy yourself.

Good care includes *you*. It includes rest, laughter, and boundaries. You can step away; it's permitted.

If you're caring for someone, remember: your wellbeing isn't selfish. It's what allows you to keep showing up for those who need you.

Self Doubt

Have you ever listened to the conversations you have with yourself? They can be ridiculous, comforting, or downright cruel. Mine were usually a bit of all three.

In my head, I was running a 24-hour radio show of 'You should do more' and 'You're not doing this right.' The self-doubt was constant. I could convince everyone else that I was coping, but not myself. Liar and my pants weren't on fire! I love that expression.

So, I focused on reading self-help books and trying meditation with more structure. At first, I was hopeless. I couldn't sit still for over two minutes without thinking about what needed to go on the shopping list or something else. But once I got the hang of it, it became one of the best things I ever did for myself. It didn't make the chaos disappear, but it gave me space to breathe. Breath work is a big topic at the moment and I think it's misunderstood. Of course we know how to breathe...check it out, it may make things a little easier for you.

The more I calmed my mind, the more I realised how much I'd been carrying. When you're in survival mode for too long, you forget what normal even feels like.

There were nights when I'd lie awake, thinking, 'What happens if something happens to me?' Who would look after them? Could I expect Sue to take this on? These thoughts terrified me.

And if I'm completely honest, there were darker thoughts too. Thoughts like, 'What if I got ill, not seriously, just enough to take me out of action for a while?' I never said it out loud, but it crossed my mind more than once. I didn't want to escape my parents; I wanted to escape the pressure. The *darkness* was daunting.

That's the kind of truth we don't like to admit. But it's real.

Dad didn't always make things easy. Sometimes when he was tired or frustrated, he'd say something that would hit me straight in the chest. Once, when I snapped at him for something minor, he said, 'Would you rather we went into a home?'

It stung. I wanted to shout 'No!' but part of me wanted to say, 'Maybe, just for a week.' The guilt that followed was instantaneous. We both knew it wasn't going to happen. I'd made a promise, and we both knew I meant it.

There were also moments of pure ridiculousness. For years I took charge of everyone's Christmas stocking. I loved choosing the right knickknacks for the right person. One year, I put a box of soaps in Dad's, three scents I approved of, nicely packaged. He opened them, frowned, and accused me of suggesting he smelled bad. He wouldn't let it lie. I lost it. Properly lost it. I shouted back, burst into tears and refused to talk to him for three weeks. This is true...three entire weeks where I refused to do more than the bare minimum of feeding him and tending only to what *needed* to be done.

That's what happens when exhaustion and self-doubt meet: you explode over soap.

I can see now that I was burned out. My confidence had disappeared. Every decision felt like life and death. I second-guessed everything, from how I helped Mum out of her chair to whether I'd cooked Dad's eggs too hard. It was a struggle.

I was living in a constant state of 'Am I doing enough?' That's a dangerous place to live.

When I could take a rare break, even just a few hours away, something positive started happening. My perspective began to change, and the fog clouding my mind cleared. I could see that I was doing more than enough, that perfection wasn't the goal. It was survival. But every time I was on my way back home, a sense of dread washed over me. I hated having to go back. Just as I feared what the conversation would be when 'Home' flashed up on my mobile.

That was the start of learning to talk to myself differently. Not kindly, not yet, but less like an enemy. It also made me answer the 'home' call with less venom in my voice.

I reminded myself that I was doing my best, even if it's messy, clumsy or a bit *sweary*, still counts.

Because it does.

Practitioner Reflection: The Inner Critic

Self-doubt thrives in silence. When you're caring for someone, your entire world shrinks to a routine, and the quiet moments may become breeding grounds for harsh thoughts.

It helps to externalise that voice. When you catch yourself thinking, "I'm failing,' ask, 'Would I say that to a friend?'

Probably not. So don't say it to yourself.

Compassion starts at home, and in grief work, we learn that self-compassion isn't indulgence. It's maintenance.

My Incident

I didn't see it coming. Not in the conscious sense, anyway. There's a little hint that things weren't so great in the last chapter, but at the same time, I thought I was making positive changes.

It was about three years into caring for Mum and Dad when everything finally caught up with me. One night, the pressure that had been quietly building for years just burst, spectacularly.

Until then, I'd prided myself on being resilient. I could handle anything. I was *Wonder Woman* with a long to-do list (and a matching pair of Converse) but even Wonder Woman needs sleep.

In the months leading up to it, I hadn't been sleeping properly. My mind raced all night, ticking through worries like a broken metronome. Money, health, work,

Mum's care, Dad's mood, the future - it was endless. And when your brain never switches off, your body falls apart. Things don't work as they're supposed to.

I was drinking more than usual, pretending it was 'a little reward.' I was running on coffee, adrenaline, alcohol and guilt. The combination proved too destructive.

The night it happened; I was out with friends at the pub. I'd been snappy all week and felt like I was about to explode, but I plastered on a smile and said, '*I was fine.*' Then someone said something insignificant; I don't even remember what. It was silly, but it was enough so send an emotional rocket through me. I broke. Surrounded by witnesses, the façade dropped, and I crumbled.

I don't remember the details. I know I shouted. I know I cried. I know I scared people who loved me. Sue was there, and she did her best to calm me down, but I was gone. Completely out of control.

The next morning, I woke up with my head pounding and my mouth tasting like something I'd rather not think about. The house was too quiet. What had I done? There wasn't the usual noise of chatter, the noise of a TV on so loud it could burst an eardrum. Sue brought me a coffee and whispered, 'You'll be okay.' That's when I realised how *not okay* I'd been for a long time.

I hid under the duvet for most of the day, too ashamed to face anyone. I'd always been the strong one, the capable one, the one holding everyone else up. But that night showed me that strength without rest isn't strength; it's survival on the edge.

It took me weeks to recover physically and mentally. For a while, I felt like a part of me was broken.

I didn't go to the doctor; I was terrified they'd offer medication, and I didn't want to be numbed. I wanted to understand what I'd experienced. So, I did what I always do: I researched, I reflected, and I tried to heal myself the only way I knew how - by being honest.

I started taking St. John's Wort. I cut back on drinking. I forced myself to sleep through meditation exercises, a pair of earplugs and an eye mask. Slowly, the fog lifted. The guilt stayed longer, but I learned to live with it.

Sue and I talked about it properly, which helped. She never made me feel like I'd failed. She just reminded me that even the strongest people break if they carry too much for too long.

That breakdown, as horrible as it was, affected me positively...*eventually.* It made me realise that burnout is a warning. You can only give so much before your body and mind wave red flags.

Now, if ever I feel myself edging towards that same cliff, I stop. I breathe. I step back. I let the world pause for a moment. Because no one gets medals for running themselves into the ground. What use would I be to anyone then? About as useful as a chocolate teapot!

Practitioner Reflection: When the Body Says 'Enough'

Burnout is not a weakness. It's the body's way of saying, 'You've gone too far without me.'
In grief and caregiving, we often ignore our own signals until something breaks.

If you recognise yourself in this story, try this:
Check in with your body before your mind.
Ask, 'What do I need right now?' If the answer is rest, or silence, or cry in the car, that's okay. That's healing.

The goal isn't to fall apart. To reach a point where you're forced into action as there's nowhere lower to go. It's knowing how to put yourself back together, gently, when you do.

Caring Without Losing Yourself

When you're caring for someone, your own needs can quietly slip to the bottom of the list, somewhere between 'find the TV remote' and 'call the GP again.' It's not because you don't matter; it's because love makes you put someone else first. But here's the truth: if you run on empty for too long, you'll have nothing left to give.

Caring is emotional work. It's also physical and mental; it pulls on every part of you. And while you can't always change the circumstances, you *can* make small choices that help you stay grounded and connected to yourself. Yes, this is easier said than done, especially when you are *existing* in the thick of it, but maybe even *one* little nugget from here will stick with you. I hope so.

1. A daily check-in with YOU

You know how we say to others, 'Are you alright?' 'How are things?' Start asking it inwardly too and be honest. Some days you'll say, 'Actually, no, I'm shattered,' and that's okay. Awareness is the first step toward balance. You can't make positive changes if you don't know they need to be made.

2. Accept help

When someone says, 'Let me know if there's anything I can do,' don't brush it off. Instead, say, 'Actually, could you pick up some milk?' or 'Would you sit with Mum for half an hour so I can get out?' People want to help; they just need to know how. (Perhaps asking them to do things like mow the lawn or do the ironing you've put off for so long is a step too far!)

3. Keep a tiny piece of your life for *yourself*

It might be a walk, a book, a few minutes of silence in the car before you go inside. Guard it like it's sacred, because it is. That small space keeps you connected to who you are beyond the caring role (I used to sit in the car at the top of the drive, not wanting to open the front door. This wasn't healthy, but the walks with Spud, our dog, were.)

4. Remember the person you care for is still *them*

It's easy to see only the illness, the frailty, the frustration, but they're still the same person beneath it. Try to find moments that remind you both of that: an old song, a shared joke, a familiar story. It helps you both hold on to dignity and connection.

5. Talk about it

You don't have to be endlessly strong or positive. Speak honestly to a friend, a counsellor, a support group, even just out loud to yourself. Words release what the heart is carrying (for me, I wrote it all down in journals. Boy, do they make painful reading now, but they let the thoughts out of my head, making space for others to creep in.)

6. Forgive yourself often

You'll lose patience. You'll feel guilty for wanting time off. You'll say the wrong thing. You'll forget something important. You're human. None of this means you're failing; it means you're doing something incredibly hard.

7. Plan little pockets of rest

You might not get a full day off, but you can have moments. A slow cup of coffee/tea by the window. Sitting outside for five minutes. Listening to your favourite song. Rest isn't always about sleep; it's about giving your nervous system a chance to breathe and reset.

8. Think ahead

At some point, caring will shift or end. That thought can bring both relief and fear. It's okay to feel both. When the time comes, your love doesn't vanish; it just changes shape. Knowing that helps ease the guilt that can follow. (At one point I thought about calling this book "*Goodness, Guilt, and Me*" and although I do still have those feelings of guilt, I no longer allow them to fester in my mind.)

Healing Work

After my breakdown, something in me shifted. It wasn't dramatic. There was no lightbulb moment of realisation. It was quieter and far less dramatic than that.

I woke up one morning and realised that the world hadn't ended. I was still here. Still breathing. Still capable of putting one foot in front of the other.

That already felt like progress.

The weeks that followed were uncomfortable. I couldn't hide behind 'being busy' anymore. I had to face myself. My limits, my needs, my guilt. I'd spent years caring for everyone else, but I'd never really learned to care for myself. Where was the girl who enjoyed dancing around the kitchen like no one was watching? Feather boa and all.

Then came a new period of *learning*.

I started with small things. Walks outside. A proper breakfast. Fifteen minutes of peace before anyone else woke up. Sometimes I'd sit in the car outside the house simply to enjoy the silence before I went in. Little pockets of space that belonged to me.

I talked more honestly about what I was feeling. This part was tough. I stopped pretending I was fine. When people asked how I was, I told the truth. 'Tired,' I'd say. Or 'angry.' Or 'grateful but hanging on by a thread.' Not that people really want you to answer that question truthfully, but it felt good to stop performing.

I started to understand that caring doesn't mean fixing. You can't patch some things up. It means showing up. Being present and taking things one day at a time. Sometimes that's enough; it's certainly a good starting point.

The more I accepted that, the more my perspective changed. I saw moments of beauty amid the hard stuff. Mum's laughter when she got the punchline before I did. Dad's gentle humour, still intact even when his body was failing him. The way Sue would catch my eye and make me laugh when things felt too heavy. We have a great relationship that's built on transparent communication. Something I value so highly.

Writing again served as therapy; it worked for me and still does. I didn't call it journaling because that sounded too organised. I just wrote what I needed to say. Pages and pages of frustration, love and exhaustion. It didn't matter if it made sense; it was a release.

That writing became the seed of this book.

In 2024, when I studied grief professionally, I finally had words for what I'd experienced. I learned about anticipatory grief, role loss, and compassion fatigue. I learned that what I felt wasn't unusual or shameful. It was human, and I was not alone.

This knowledge didn't erase the pain, but it reframed it. It gave me a language to use where before there had only been noise.

Caring for my parents broke me open in ways I didn't expect, but it also made me who I am. The experience stripped everything unnecessary away. It taught me empathy, patience, and the power of showing up when things are uncomfortable.

I see grief as a kind of teacher. It's brutal, yes, but it's also honest. It forces you to look at what really matters. It holds up a mirror and asks, 'Who are you now?'

And slowly, I answered that question.

Practitioner Reflection: Healing Isn't a Straight Line

Recovery from grief and burnout doesn't look neat. It's not a ladder you climb; it's more like a tide, coming in and out, sometimes calm, sometimes wild.

Healing begins with permission.

Permission to stop pretending.

Permission to rest.

Permission to laugh again without guilt.

If you've been through a loss, try to notice the small signs of healing. The first time you sleep through the night. The first time you make a plan that's just for you. The first time you talk about them, and it makes you smile instead of cry.

That's the work. That's the healing.

The Goodbye Years

Learning to Let Go

The last few years with Mum and Dad were both the hardest and the most precious of my life. We knew time was running out, even if no one ever said it out loud. It hung in the air like a truth we didn't want to refer to. Knowing that the inevitable would happen didn't make it *real* for me. You see, running on autopilot shielded me from the reality of all that was happening around us.

Two years before they died, my Dad was rushed into hospital and we were told that he wouldn't make it. I remember standing by his bedside feeling numb. No emotion. Why couldn't I *feel* anything? The doctor asked about a DNR (Do Not Resuscitate) and I didn't know what he was talking about. Dad overheard and was adamant it *wasn't his time to go.* The doctor took me aside and *advised* me to speak to Dad as it was unlikely he would survive the night. You already know that he lasted much longer than one more night! Call me sentimental, but I truly believe he didn't want to die before the love of his life!

Mum's strength was fading, but her mind remained sharp. Her eyes still full of mischief, but her body couldn't keep up. She'd still boss me around with a blink or a raised eyebrow, and somehow that made it easier to pretend that everything was normal. Dad's movement became more restricted until he couldn't even make it into the kitchen to make tea. He'd doze off in his chair with the TV on, pretending he was 'just resting his eyes.' He was still funny, still proud, but more fragile than I'd ever seen him.

We all became experts at pretending everything was fine. We talked about what to have for dinner instead of what the future would bring. We told jokes when we really wanted to cry. That's how we as a family survived the long goodbye - with denial, humour and the occasional gin and tonic.

I stopped measuring time in days (or sleeps) and started measuring it in moments. A smile. A good meal. A minor victory like getting through a day without panic. The time when the four of us went out to lunch in various styles of Superdry coats - functional, bright and not frumpy. There was no way my parents were going to look frumpy. The time I had to leave the car in town because Mum and I went out for lunch, and I ended up on the cocktails and Mum on the mocktails. The looks she gave people in shops who looked through her as though she was invisible. Those became the markers that mattered. The *little* things.

When you've cared for someone for so long, you simultaneously live in two worlds. In one, you're managing medication, appointments and endless paperwork. In the other, you're already grieving them, quietly, while trying to live your own life.

I didn't want to imagine life without them, so I focused on the present. The smell of Mum's perfume. The sound of Dad's slippers shuffling down the hall. The little domestic details that don't seem important until they're gone.

When Mum died, it was peaceful. The moment you can't prepare for, even when you've seen it coming for years. There was a change in her focus in the weeks leading up to that day, and I was told by a doctor to call the family round. (I'd been there before, so I wasn't convinced.) I did as I was told, and for the last time, all four of Mum's children were in the same place.

The doctor suggested Mum should go to the hospital; and I saw the look of pure panic in Mum's eyes. I asked what it would take to keep her at home. The doctor was brilliant. She completed a safeguarding assessment and told me she would make sure this happened. We did what it took. It was hard. She was in pain, and we had a hotline number to call out medical professionals during the night to administer pain relief. One morning, I called the number at 3am and within an hour, two nurses arrived. Standing in the hallway, one of them wrapped her arms around me and gave me such a warm hug. I melted into that hug. Mum was hanging in there, and I truly believe that she waited a few extra days to make sure she didn't leave us on one of the three birthdays that fell around that time.

The last time I looked into her eyes and *saw* her is a moment I will never forget. Then, for the last 36 hours of her life, she lay peacefully. The pain was gone. I sat with her and held her hand and told her she'd done enough. She'd given enough. And she had. Dad and I were with her, and the last thing she heard was us laughing...all over the positioning of her dentures and the threat that she'd bite Dad if he tried to move them. It wasn't cruel laughter, but a moment shared between two of the people who meant the most to her in the world. Then, she was gone.

Three months later, Dad followed her. It felt cruel, but also right. They'd been together for over fifty years. One couldn't have stayed without the other. Dad only stayed for those months because I hadn't told him he could go. The Doctor pointed out that it had come from me; I was the one who needed to let him, that he was waiting for my permission. 'I'll be okay, Dad.' I said, without understanding the poignancy of that moment. A few hours later, he was gone.

The house was suddenly silent. I still caught myself listening for them - the sound of the kettle, the oxygen machine that dominated the silence, Mum's soft giggle from the living room. Grief is full of echoes like that.

The day after my Dad's funeral, I stood in the kitchen and realised there was nothing left to *do*. For years my life had revolved around their needs. Suddenly, there were no lists, no appointments, no one to check on. I didn't know what to do with the silence.

That's the strange part of losing someone after caring for them for so long. It's not just their absence you have to face; it's the collapse of purpose. You lose your role. Your reason. Your rhythm.

It took me a long time to understand that grief isn't about filling that space. It's about learning to accept it into your life.

So, I started with the small things again. A walk. A hot bath. Writing. Remembering. Breathing. Letting the quiet slowly become something I could live inside, instead of something I feared.

I still talk to them. I still say goodnight. Sometimes I still ask for their advice. I don't hear answers, but I always feel their presence.

It was during the three months between them dying that my professional life took an unexpected shift. As I stood behind the lectern delivering my Mum's tribute, a sense of calm washed over me and I found myself drawn to working as a funeral celebrant, which I pursued with a deeper passion than anything I'd done before... and six years later, I still do.

Practitioner Reflection: The Space After

When someone we love dies, the world goes still. For carers, that stillness can feel unbearable. For so long, your life has been about someone else's comfort, safety, survival. When that ends, so does part of your identity.

This is where the next phase of grief begins, not letting go, but learning to stay connected differently.

Try this:

Light a candle and talk to them.

Write them a letter about something that happened today.

Keep the connection but release the duty.

You cared. You showed up. You loved well. That's enough.

Life After Death

When the sympathy cards stopped arriving and everyone went back to their normal lives, I was still standing in the same kitchen, wondering what to do next.

For years, my life had been one long list of responsibilities. Suddenly, there was no one to care for. No one asking for tea, no carers to let in, no reason to get up at 6 a.m. The silence was deafening.

People say, 'You must be relieved to have your life back.' But I didn't know what that meant anymore. My life had tied itself to theirs for so long that I didn't know where they ended and I began.

In the first few weeks after Dad died, I felt like I was walking around without skin. Everything hurt. The smallest things set me off - the smell of Mum's hand cream, the sight of Dad's favourite mug in the cupboard. I couldn't throw anything away. Not yet.

The house was full of ghosts, but thankfully not the spooky kind. The gentle everyday kind memories. The ones that make you smile and cry at the same time.

I thought I'd feel free when the caring stopped, but I didn't. I felt lost. Grief had no schedule and no map, and I needed to learn to navigate my path again.

So, I continued writing. I wrote about them, about me, about the strange in-between of losing your parents and finding yourself. The words came as they had before, messy and unfiltered, but this time they felt different. They weren't just about survival anymore. They were about understanding. I wrote poems, some of which I read during their funerals. They captured moments and sentiments that were personal to me and to them. Two years later, I published my first poetry book, *Moments in Time,* which was also influenced by my gaining experience in the funeral industry. They are not great works of art, but they acknowledge the importance of treasuring memories in the simplest of ways.

That writing became my way home. It gave shape to the chaos. It helped me make sense of the years I'd spent running on empty.

I started seeing friends again. Slowly. Carefully. People didn't always know what to say, and I learned that was okay. I didn't need perfect words. I just needed company. Sue never tried to fix things; she just sat with me as the tears fell, or when the silence took over. I also had to remember that she was hurting too.

Grief has a way of rearranging your life. It takes what mattered before and throws it in the air. When it all lands again, the pieces look different.

I realised I didn't want to go back to who I had been before. I wanted to take what I'd learned and use it. And I did. I trained as a grief practitioner. I wanted to understand grief better, not set up a business.

Learning the theory after living the reality was both comforting and confronting. There were moments when the textbooks made me cry, because I recognised myself in the case studies. But I also found hope there, that pain can become a purpose. I use some of what I learned in my role as a celebrant. I meet people when the death of a loved one is so raw, sometimes within days of them dying.

That's what "life after' became for me. A continuation, not a replacement. A life built around learning how to adapt when the world changes beyond recognition.

I started helping others through their losses, the funerals, the goodbyes, the unbearable days that follow. Every time I stand beside someone who's grieving, I think of Mum and Dad. They taught me how to show up with love, how to listen without fixing, and how to laugh when life feels impossible.

They're in everything I do now.

In every ceremony.

In every quiet conversation after the service.

In every moment of grace that follows grief.

Life after loss isn't about moving on. It's about moving forward with what remains. And what remained for me was love that directed me on a fresh path in life, one that I treasure.

Practitioner Reflection: The Rebuilding

After a loss, we often search for the person we were before. But that version of us is gone, and that's okay. Grief transforms us.

The goal isn't to go back. It's to rebuild. To find a life that can hold both the sadness and the joy.

If you're in that space, ask yourself:

What have I learned about love?

What still brings me peace?

What do I want to carry forward?

When you answer those questions, you'll find that the life you're building isn't smaller than before; it's deeper.

The Gifts of Grief

It took me a long time to use the words *grief* and *gift* in the same sentence. For a while, it felt almost offensive to do so. How could something that hurts so much possibly hold anything good?

But it does. And that's the strange, unexpected truth I've discovered.

Grief stripped me bare. It peeled away everything that wasn't essential. The noise, the nonsense, the pretending - all gone. What was left was *real*.

It taught me patience. Not the 'waiting for the kettle to boil' kind, but the deep, soul-level patience that comes from accepting that life doesn't follow your plans.

It taught me empathy. I used to listen to people out of politeness. Now I listen to *hear* them. When someone talks about their pain, I don't rush to fix it. I just sit in it with them, because I know that's what helps.

It taught me humour. Real, black, belly-aching humour that sneaks up in the middle of the saddest days. The kind that saves you. Mum would have loved that part. She'd be the first to say that laughter belongs in every room, even the quiet ones.

Grief also taught me gratitude, not in a forced 'count your blessings' way, but in the quiet noticing. The sun on the washing line. A song on the radio. The smell of cut grass. Ordinary moments that somehow feel like miracles when you've seen how fragile everything is.

Most of all, grief taught me a deeper understanding of love. Not the easy kind, but the authentic kind. The kind that stays when people are gone, that shapes how you live, that refuses to fade.

I wouldn't wish what I've been through on anyone. But I also wouldn't trade what I've learned from it. Grief gave me perspective. It gave me purpose. It gave me a deeper sense of who I am and what truly matters.

That's why I call them the gifts of grief. They don't come wrapped in bows. They arrive subtly, often after tears, but they change you in ways nothing else can.

If you're in the middle of grief, I want you to know this: you won't stay there forever. The pain won't always feel this sharp. One day, without realising it, you'll laugh again. You'll notice the world looking beautiful. You'll carry your person with you, not as a weight, but as a warmth.

And that's when you'll see it - the gift.

"How lucky am I to have something that makes saying goodbye so hard," A. A. Milne

Practitioner Reflection: The Integration

The end of grief isn't forgetting. It's integration, accepting loss as part of your story.

In grief practice, it's called 'continuing bonds.' It means your relationship with the person doesn't end when they die. It changes form.

You carry them forward through stories, habits, traditions and love.

If you're finding your way through grief, ask yourself:

How do I still feel connected to them?

What do I want to keep alive in their memory?

Grief's greatest gift is that it reminds us we're capable of deep love. And that love doesn't die.

Goodness, Grief, and Me

When I first started writing my story, I thought it was about loss. Now I see it was always about love.

Love in all its glory; the deep kind, the complicated kind and the kind that drives you to behave in ways you never imagined. The kind that holds your hand in hospital corridors, that makes endless cups of tea, that finds humour in the worst moments. The kind that refuses to give up, even when you're exhausted.

When grief arrives, it changes everything. How you adapt to the change gives you a deeper understanding of this experience that connects us all at some point.

I used to think of grief as a dark, heavy thing that you just had to get through. But now, after years of living with it, I see it as something more like weather. Some days it's a drizzle, other days it's a full-blown storm, and sometimes it surprises you with sunlight. You can't control it. You just learn to carry an umbrella and get on with it.

There are still moments when it catches me off guard. A smell, a song, a sentence. The sight of someone wearing Mum's favourite shade of lipstick. The sound of a man laughing in the same way as my Dad. It happens, and I let it. I've learned not to fight it anymore.

Because this is the truth no one tells you, grief doesn't go away. It grows around you. It softens. It becomes part of who you are.

And strangely, that's comforting.

When I look back now, I don't see just the pain. I see everything else that came with it. If there's one thing I know for sure, it's that grief isn't the end of the story. It's the middle, the part that changes everything, but not the part that defines you forever.

I thought I'd never feel whole again after losing my parents. But I am whole. Different, yes, but still whole. They're part of that wholeness. I see them everywhere - in the kindness of strangers, in the strength of the families I now help, and in the small, everyday moments that remind me of home.

That's the 'goodness' in *Goodness, Grief, and Me*. It's not about pretending everything's fine. It's about finding meaning in the mess. It's about looking at the hardest thing you've ever survived and saying, 'I'm still here, and I'm still me.'

So, if you're reading this and you're in that place - the raw, aching, how-do-I-breathe place, hold on. One day, you'll sit where I am now and realise that you've carried your grief far enough to see what's beyond it.

You'll find goodness again. You'll find yourself again. And that, my friend, is where the healing begins.

Practitioner Reflection: The Full Circle

Grief doesn't end. It evolves. It becomes a quiet companion instead of a constant ache.

The work of grief is not to let go of love, but to let go of fear - the fear that you'll never feel joy again, or that moving forward means leaving them behind.

In truth, you carry them with you into everything that comes next. That's the circle. That's the gift.

"They are with you still, in every quiet moment, in every kind act, in every burst of laughter that comes from nowhere." Hilary Steel.

A Note from Me to You

If you've made it this far, thank you. Really. I know that reading about grief isn't easy. It asks you to sit with feelings most people spend their lives trying to avoid. But if you're still here, it means something in these pages resonated. Maybe you've loved and lost too. Maybe you're caring for someone right now. Or maybe you just needed to know you're not the only one who's felt this kind of ache.

Whatever brought you here, I hope it helps you.

This book helped me to heal parts of myself that I didn't know were still broken. But more than that, it reminded me how powerful stories are, especially the honest ones. Grief doesn't like perfection; it likes truth.

And the truth is, you don't 'get over' grief. You learn to live with it. You build a life around it.
You laugh again, love again, grow again, not despite it, but alongside it.

If you're still in the thick of it, please remember this: you are doing better than you think.
That you're reading this, breathing through the pain, shows strength you probably don't even see yet.

Keep talking. Keep remembering. Keep finding the small moments that remind you that life, even in its messiest form, is still worth living.

And when you can, tell your story. Someone out there needs to hear it, just like you needed to hear mine.

Goodness, grief, and me - and now, goodness, grief, and you.

With love,

Hilary

Practical Exercises

Practical Exercises

I thought that studying to be a grief practitioner would help further my understanding when visiting families to arrange funeral services. What I didn't realise was that I was also giving myself the very tools I needed to help with my own healing. This really came to light when my brother Lindsay died, and I couldn't attend the funeral. Each of the lessons here is a reflective exercise and requires you to be honest with yourself.

This section gathers some practices that proved to be most valuable, both personally and professionally. This is not about 'getting over grief' - we already understand that doesn't happen, because grief remains a part of you. It lives alongside us, and for me, sometimes it's sad, and sometimes it's humour that pulls me through. I often tell families it's 'never the big things that have the most weight' in times of sadness. It's true. All the memories that make me smile are of much happier times.

Here you'll find exercises designed to help you pause, take a step back and pay attention to what's really happening in your head and heart. Some invite you to write things down, and I've left space if you wish to keep everything in this book. Some are for your own reflection, and some will hopefully inspire you to take little bits of action. There is no right or wrong way to work through these exercises. All I ask is that you be honest with yourself.

Take what helps you and leave what doesn't. Even in the most confusing moments of grief, healing is possible. Just take it one step at a time and be kind to yourself.

A Comfort Check In

This is an exercise that helps you check in with where you are right now.

Grab your 'comfort' drink, find a quiet space and ask yourself:

- What hurts right now?
- What makes you feel better?

- What can you leave until tomorrow? Next week?
- What needs to be done now?

Understanding what you are feeling *in the moment* helps you to focus on one thing at a time, both emotionally and physically.

Notes

Letters Unsent

It's common to have unfinished business with the people we love who've died. This is a gentle exercise to acknowledge unspoken words. It involves writing a letter to the person who's died, without thinking about it too much. No filter and no editing. Tell them everything you wish you'd said, including things that may seem negative. This isn't about being poetic; it's about honesty. Once you've written it, you don't even have to read it back; burn it if you wish. The important thing is to get these words out in the open. Obviously, if you use the space below to write your letter, don't burn the book!

Dear..........

Honesty and Happiness Jar Ritual

Even when you're in the thick of grief, there are still things to be thankful for. Finding these brief glimmers of hope can lift a little weight. The jar doesn't have to be physical, but the idea is to fill it up with positive thoughts and actions.

Every day, write one thing that's positive, both big and small. A happy memory, an act of kindness, a smell that brings comfort (perfume, rain on concrete) anything that brings a little peace - and pop it in the 'jar.'

When the 'jar' is full, tip it out. This serves as a reminder that things aren't always as bad as we make them out to be.

A Conversation with Yourself

When you are truly honest with yourself, a new perspective on things can help you heal. Tapping into your subconscious is where the magic can happen. You already know that you've been through a lot, which is what brought you to this book, but you're still here, which means there's a part of you that wants to feel better.

I found this difficult after my 'incident' but by going through this, I know how much lighter I felt on the other side.

Look at yourself in the mirror and tell yourself, 'You've been through a lot, but here you are, still standing.' Now, write the thoughts that come to you. Notice whether you phrase things in a negative or positive way. For example, 'I may be standing but only just' or 'I've come this far and want to ease the pain.'

How we form sentences tells a lot about ourselves. If you notice you veer towards the *negative*, try saying the same thing in a more positive way.

Now think about the way you would talk to a friend if they were in your position. What would you *think* of the way they talk to themselves? Be as kind to yourself as you would be to them.

Notes

Staying Connected

Just because someone is no longer with us doesn't mean we have to wipe all traces of them away. There's a myth surrounding grief about 'letting go' or 'moving on'- often this is said in relation to gaining 'closure.' I think 'closure' misleads us in the grieving process. It's final, but love continues.

When someone dies, we don't 'let them go.' Not really. What we need to learn are new ways to stay connected.

Studying grief showed me that many of the people I spoke to felt guilty for wanting to stay connected. Exactly the opposite of 'letting go.' They'd say things like, 'I know I should move on'– why? Move on from what exactly? Learn to adapt, yes. Staying connected is healthy and comforting. Because that person is no longer here doesn't mean we have to forget the impact they had on us when they were alive.

Here are a few suggestions that might help you during this phase of your grief.

· Acknowledge anniversaries in your own way. Celebrate them if it feels right. Light a candle, go to a favourite place you enjoyed together or simply allow yourself time to sit and think about them.

· Talk about them, remember those times that made you smile, and thank them for all they mean to you.

· Talk to them, either out loud or by writing it down. Express what you're feeling; tell them things about your day that you would have done in person.

· Create a playlist of music you both enjoyed. Yes, this might be painful, but it can also help to open your mind to why each track holds meaning.

Notes

The Letter

I wrote this letter two years after my parents died and it was included in my initial *ramblings.* I've kept this true to the original.

Dear Mum and Dad,

It's been two years since you both took your final breath, and I want to tell you that I'm sorry.

This isn't one of those throwaway apologies for nicking the last packet of crisps or coming home late. It's deeper than that. Painful, even. You're not here for me to hand this letter to, but I need to acknowledge how much our shared years have shaped me — how profoundly you've left your mark.

I remember the freedom of my childhood — the way mistakes were never held against me, just gently learned from. You gave me a wonderful start in life, full of love, laughter, and adventure. You both worked so hard to make sure we never went without. Family holidays abroad, clubs, hobbies — your attitude was always "try it, and if you love it, stick at it."

Mum, you'd sit in the car while I went off for extra violin lessons after orchestra practice. You both supported every mad idea I had. And though I got teased at school for having parents closer in age to my friends' grandparents, I never cared. You were cooler than most of their mums and dads put together. You let me stay out late and have parties — though maybe that was down to experience after raising three kids before me. There wasn't much I could have done to shock you!

You always made me feel safe. Whether in person or just through a phone call.

Later, when I became your carer, that word *'Home'* flashing up on my phone started to make my heart sink. Sometimes I'd resent those calls — to pick something up, to come help, to rush home. I'm sorry for that. Sorry that I felt it, and sorrier still if you ever sensed it. It was selfish of me, and I know it must have hurt.

Mum, I'm sorry I didn't take better care of your clothes. They weren't always organised as you liked, and I know it frustrated you when you couldn't tell the carers exactly what you wanted to wear. You asked so many times for me to go through that red suitcase on top of the wardrobe. I didn't — not until it was time to give it all away. That one stings.

Dad, I'm grateful you discovered online shopping. It saved me from many a hopeless wander around DIY stores. You found clever gadgets to make life easier — like that battery pack for Mum's wheelchair. Your resourcefulness always amazed me. It reminded me of when you first found QVC after your stroke in 1994 — Mum would only have to *mention* she liked something, and it'd turn up a few days later. She learned to stop mentioning things pretty fast!

I know Mum needed more hands-on care, and I'm sorry you didn't get quite the same level of attention, Dad. But Sue and I did everything we could to keep you comfortable and loved. I know you appreciated it, but still... it weighs on me. Even now. Maybe one day that guilt will soften.

Thank you both for welcoming Sue into our family so openly. You treated her like another daughter, and I'll always treasure that. Those lunches we had — the four of us and Spud — were golden. I still laugh thinking of us all bundled in our Superdry coats like a walking advert. Even Spud had his bright bandanna on. You always made an entrance.

It became harder to take you out once the oxygen came into play, and I know I snapped sometimes. I'm sorry. Watching you both decline broke me in ways I didn't want to admit. I was angry at losing you — even before you'd gone. You were so poorly, yet you stayed strong. Still taking care of your girls. Still protecting us. You were a gentleman and a gentle man, Dad. I'll always be proud to be your daughter.

I remember your last wedding anniversary — Dad, you weren't well, but Mum wanted one last outing. Sue and I took the day off and took her into town. She had a little lager, laughed, ate well — it felt almost normal again. I went back to that pub recently and sat at the same table. In my mind, you were both there — Mum in her chair, Spud by her side, all of us laughing. Within five months, you were both gone.

Thank you for trusting me with your final, precious moments.

Thank you for being the best parents I could ever have wished for.

Looking back now, I see all the love, the patience, the unwavering support — and I'm grateful beyond words.

There's so much more I could say, but it hurts knowing you'll never actually read this. That's when it really hits — you're not coming home. Still, your strength inspires me. It pushes me to turn this pain, this experience, into something that might one day help others.

Sleep tight, my beautiful parents.

With all my love,

Your pain-in-the-arse daughter,

Hils xx

What 'Now' Looks Like

If someone had told me years ago that grief would lead me here — to a life built around helping others through their own loss - I probably would've laughed, or cried, or both. Yet here I am, standing in front of families, telling stories of lives lived and loved, knowing how it feels on the inside of what they're going through.

Life after grief isn't what I imagined. It's quieter, simpler, softer in places, and stronger in others. The laughter comes easier now. The tears still appear sometimes too, but they've learned to share space with joy. Mum and Dad are never far away - they're in the way I comfort families, in the words I write, in the lessons I pass on. They taught me that love doesn't die with the person; it just finds a new way to show up.

My brother Lindsay died while I was working on this book, and sadly, I don't feel that I have closure. Sibling loss hits you differently, and I've made a promise to myself to take a leaf out of my book, literally, and allow myself to come to terms with it.

Sue and I live a life filled with gratitude, with space for stillness, and with enough humour to carry us through the odd wobbly day. I no longer rush through life ticking boxes. I pause. I notice. And together; we go out for walks with Spud. Time is what we cherish, and finding value in the little things makes life seem so much smoother.

The goodness in *Goodness, Grief, and Me* isn't about pretending it's all fine. It's about finding meaning in the moments that come after the hardest ones, the morning light through the curtains, a smile you didn't expect, a story that makes you laugh even when it hurts. It's about knowing that grief changes you, but it doesn't have to break you.

If you're reading this and wondering when it gets easier, the answer is...slowly. But it does. And one day, you'll wake up, pour your coffee, and realise you've learned to live again, not instead of the love you lost, but because of it.

That's the goodness. That's the gift.

Hilary x

My life is still chaotic, in a different way, so if you'd like to connect with me, the Facebook page **Hilary Steel – Celebrant** is where I share random things, including poems in relation to grief and @Hilaryjsteel on Instagram is where I hang out for all my roles in life. I hope to see you over there...

Acknowledgements

To Mum and Dad, Harry and Jennifer Steel - you taught me what love looks like in action.

To Sue, my constant, my laughter, my calm. You've seen every version of me, and you stayed.

To my family and friends, the ones who kept showing up even when I disappeared into the chaos, thank you for your patience, your messages, your meals, and your humour. You probably saved me more times than I've admitted.

To the families I've since had the privilege of supporting in their own grief. Thank you for trusting me with your stories.

And finally, to every carer, daughter, son, partner, or friend who's ever whispered, *'I can't do this anymore,'* and then got up and did it anyway - this book is for you.

Quick References

To Mum and Dad, Harry and Jennifer Steel - you taught me what love looks like in action.

To Sue, my constant, my laughter, my calm. You've seen every version of me, and you stayed.

To my family and friends, the ones who kept showing up even when I disappeared into the chaos, thank you for your patience, your messages, your meals, and your humour. You probably saved me more times than I've admitted.

To the families I've since had the privilege of supporting in their own grief. Thank you for trusting me with your stories.

And finally, to every carer, daughter, son, partner, or friend who's ever whispered, *'I can't do this anymore,'* and then got up and did it anyway - this book is for you.

About the author

Hilary Steel is a funeral celebrant, writer, grief practitioner, and self-confessed people-watcher with a love for storytelling and a knack for finding humour even in life's messiest moments.

After caring for both of her parents through their final years, Hilary's perspective on life, love, and loss shifted forever. Wanting to understand more about the emotional terrain of grief — and how we can live alongside it — she trained as a grief practitioner and began writing *Goodness, Grief, and Me*, a book that blends honesty, warmth, and practical wisdom for anyone navigating life after loss.

Hilary's work as a celebrant is known for its humanity and heart — she has written and delivered hundreds of funerals across Kent, helping families find words when theirs have gone missing. Her natural style combines compassion with curiosity, a touch of irreverence, and a belief that love doesn't end — it simply changes shape.

When she isn't writing or standing at the front of a service, you'll find Hilary hosting the **Kent Women in Business Awards**, the **Kent Hair, Health, and Beauty Awards** or simply reading a book.

Goodness, Grief, and Me is her first non-fiction book — written not as an expert talking down, but as a fellow traveller who knows that sometimes, the only way through grief... is to keep talking, keep laughing, and keep topping up the bird feeder.

The page Hilary Steel – Celebrant on Facebook is where I share random things, including poems in relation to grief. @Hilaryjsteel on Instagram is where I hang out for all my roles in life. I hope to see you over there...

Printed in Dunstable, United Kingdom

73830066R00078